365 ways to survive as a parent

JULIET JANVRIN

LION
Publishing

Text copyright © 2000 Juliet Janvrin
Illustrations copyright © 2000 Stephanie Strickland
This edition copyright © 2000 Lion Publishing

The moral rights of the author and illustrator
have been asserted

Published by
Lion Publishing plc
Sandy Lane West, Oxford, England
www.lion-publishing.co.uk
ISBN 0 7459 4285 7

First edition 2000
10 9 8 7 6 5 4 3 2 1 0

Acknowledgments

35, 36, 95, 197, 217, 329, 351: Matthew 18:10,
Ephesians 6:4 (paraphrased), Luke 18:17,
Proverbs 22:6, Proverbs 31:28, Psalm 127:3,
Matthew 19:14, from the Good News Bible
published by The Bible Societies/HarperCollins
Publishers Ltd, UK © American Bible Society
1966, 1971, 1976, 1992, used with permission.

A catalogue record for this book is available
from the British Library

Typeset in 20/20 Kidprint
Printed and bound in Italy

For
Alice
Edmund
Jack
David
and
Charlie

👎 1 👍
Parenting is not a job
from which you can become redundant.

☞ **2** ☜

Parenting is a lifetime's work contract without a pension at the end; but it's full of job satisfaction none the less.

☞ **3** ☜

A baby's cry cuts through the night like a knife.

👎 **4** 👍

The newly expectant parent-to-be says,
'This baby is not going to make a
difference to the way we live our lives.'
The experienced parent smiles gently
and says nothing.

👎 **5** 👍

Bedtime is the oldest argument in the world.

6

A child's first step
is a step into the future.

7

It's easy to judge other people's
children – but unwise to do so.

8

Only parents hear the urgency
of their baby's cry.

9

The 5.30 a.m. treat of breakfast in bed –
lukewarm tea and extremely soggy toast –
has to be eaten.

☞10👍

A baby's *fragility* is his *strength*.
It arouses all our protective instincts.

☞11👍

Children must *be* allowed to play
without adult intervention, or their
imaginations will never be stretched.

👎12👍

Parents worry about money.
Children worry about whether
the toy shop is open.

👎13👍

Parenting raises many questions,
but not many parents with answers.

👎 14 👍
The early years pass so fast.
Never wish them away.

👎 15 👍
A parent's large hand encompassing
a child's tiny one: an image of safety,
nurture and protection.

👎 16 👍

For children, the fridge is
the most opened door in life.

☞ 17 ☜
Harness the energy of
the average three-year-old
and you could run the world
for the rest of time.

☞ 18 ☜
There is no perfume more intoxicating
than a *baby freshly laundered and fed.*

☜19☞
A parent is a sandbank
that holds back the tide of life
until the child is ready to swim.

☜20☞
Grandparents offer a listening
and sympathetic ear when parents
are too busy with the noise of life.

👎 21 👍

Parents want their children to
be successful on the sports field.
They don't want to see them trampled
underfoot – by someone else's kid.

👎 22 👍

When a child asks for a pet,
make sure you're prepared
to clean out the cage.

👎 **23** 👍

The greatest security for children
is to have parents who invest in
their own relationship.

👎 **24** 👍

Children will sometimes bring
us pain and disappointment;
and comfort is hard to find.

👎 **25** 👍

Tidiness is not a priority of childhood.

👎 **26** 👍

The burden of being unforgiven
is too heavy for young shoulders.

👎 **27** 👍

Divided parents confuse children.
It is sometimes more important
to be united than to be right.

👎 **28** 👍

Children surprise us
with their unconditional love.

☞29☜

If you don't have the answers to all
the Whys, your child will ask, 'Why not?'

☞30☜

The looks and mannerisms of
family members, past and present,
pass across the face of a growing
child, startling us with their familiarity.

👎 **31** 👍

A handy excuse for when your
child's behaviour lets you down:
'He's probably tired.'

👎 **32** 👍

Babies love a routine – once you
have persuaded them to get into one.

☜33☝

It is only when you are pregnant
yourself that you find a world full
of pregnant women wherever you go.

👎 **34** 👍

Every nappy changed
is a step away from *babyhood*.

👎 **35** 👍

Jesus said, 'See that you don't despise
any of these little ones. Their angels
in heaven, I tell you, are always in the
presence of my Father in heaven.'

FROM THE NEW TESTAMENT GOSPEL OF MATTHEW

👎 36 👍

The Bible also says, 'Parents,
do not exasperate your children.'
Good advice not always followed.

👎 37 👍

To carry a child on your hip
is to carry treasure by your side.

👎 **38** 👍
To conceive a child
is to touch the future.

👎 **39** 👍
A child without discipline
will fight our failure to set
boundaries by behaving badly.

👎**40**👍

It's amazing how an appointment
with the doctor will cure a sick child,
as the receptionist who just managed
to fit her in glares at you.

👎**41**👍

As the child enters the school gates
he leaves babyhood behind.

👎 **42** 👍

Everything and anything pertaining
to babies is an interesting topic
for the new parent.

👎 **43** 👍

Do not mock children for their
wild imaginations. They are the
seedbeds of creativity.

👎44👍

A father, a mother and God can provide the three strands of a rope which will support the growing child.

👎 **45** 👍

A sleeping child is peace personified.

👎 **46** 👍

Teenagers want a parent who
is able to be a friend, but also
a reliable, authoritative figure.

👎 **47** 👍

The words 'bath time' herald the end of
the day and a chance to sit down at last.

👎 **48** 👍

Calm words... calm children.

👎 **49** 👍

A child must leave a parent
in order to grow up, but it is a
painful wrench for both of them.

☞50☜
A teenage daughter seems to have to
find many aspects of her father ridiculous
before she can make sense of another man.

☞51☜
Children have an alarming propensity
to grow out of everything.

👎 52 👍

The naked baby flails his limbs
in fear at the enormity of the world –
especially when he has his first few baths.

👎53👍
Children between the ages
of three and eleven firmly
believe in gender differences.

👎54👍
Empty promises undermine
a child's trust.

👎 55 👍
To learn to read is to discover
a pleasure that will last a lifetime.

👎 56 👍
Children paint wrinkles
on your face year by year,
whatever magic cream you use.

ᑦ57ᑫ

A wild child must be tamed,
or he will be trapped in
a cage of your making.

ᑦ58ᑫ

Teenage girls find long hair an
asset. It's brilliant to flick in
disgust at a parental comment.

👎 **59** 👍

Children who are protected from challenges
will not develop strategies to deal with life.

👎 **60** 👍

A parent of a young child has to get used
to never being alone – even in the loo!

👎 **61** 👍

The baby sleeping on your shoulder
is part of the world's future.

62

The school playground is a jungle.

☞ 63 ☜

The first movements of the baby
within the womb are like a butterfly
fluttering against your heart.

☞ 64 ☜

The labour of childhood is lightened
by the anticipation of joy.

👎 65 👍

Parents create happy Christmas memories for their children – mainly through hard work and total exhaustion.

👎 66 👍

It is best to give children strategies to cope with difficulties, rather than to placate them with soothing words.

☞67☜

The mementoes of babyhood and youth
are amongst our most precious possessions.

☞68☜

Babies love being swaddled tightly in a shawl.
It recreates the security of the womb.

👎 69 👍

Never underestimate your
importance as a parent.

👎 70 👍

Through play, a child discovers
the mysteries of the world.

Grandparents and young babies
seem to recognize one another as allies.

👎72👍
'Don't care' probably does... very much.

👎73👍
Taking your firstborn home
is a journey to a different land.

👎74👍
Being impossible is probably
best done in early childhood.

👎 **75** 👍

Children must sail beyond the
horizon their parents can see.

👎 **76** 👍

Children are born with the full
gamut of feelings and emotions.
They have not been anaesthetized
by the experience of life.

👎 **77** 👍

If our expectations are too high,
our children cannot help but fail us.

👎 **78** 👍

If our expectations are too low,
our children will become discouraged
and lack the motivation to succeed.

👎 **79** 👍

Children will eat things at
other people's houses that they
categorically refuse in their own.

👎 **80** 👍

The whining of a child drips
into the mind like water
from a *broken tap*.

👎 **81** 👍

Don't try to force your child into
the wrong shape in the postbox of life.

👎 82 👍

Computers and television were not designed to raise children.

👎 83 👍

Children and animals have a natural affinity when it comes to play rather than responsibility.

👎**84**👍

Guilt is the constant companion
of the working mother.

👎**85**👍

Children's dreams encapsulate
their fears and hopes. Take time
to listen to them.

👎86👍

Encourage children to pursue sport.
It brings fitness and health –
and expends endless energy.

👎87👍

If we don't provide children with
a spiritual and moral framework,
they will go in search of their own.

👎**88**👍

Be sure of your opinions. Teenagers
are quick to spot inconsistencies.

👎**89**👍

Imaginative children, with minds full of
ideas, are often asked to play, especially
when they can entertain their friends
without the need for adult intervention.

👎90👍

Remember, it is your son or daughter playing in the match – not you.

👍 91 👍

To overfeed a child is to risk leaving
them open to bullying and unhappiness.

👎 92 👍

Time spent with a child is
like money saved in a bank:
your investment will grow year by year.

👎 93 👍

Children hear tone, not words.

👎 94 👍

We are enchanted when a baby starts
to crawl, but soon realize that we must
reorganize our entire house to accommodate
this danger-seeking creature.

👎 95 👍

Jesus said, 'Whoever does not receive
the Kingdom of God like a child will
never enter it.'

FROM THE NEW TESTAMENT GOSPEL OF LUKE

👎 96 👍

Never leave a child crying in the night.

👎 97 👍

Children are suspicious of food –
especially when it is coloured green.

👎 98 👍

The enthusiastic and grateful child is
a first choice to take on trips; they
make all the exhaustion worthwhile.

The first steps of the toddler are a shared triumph.

👎 **100** 👍

Take time to listen to your child
at the end of the day.

👎 **101** 👍

The shadows of a nightmare are
best dispelled by the gentle light
of parental reassurance.

👎 102 👍

Children are not yet interested in our past. They are more concerned with their future.

👎 103 👍

Children are a life's work.

☞104☜
Children love new shoes.
They are proof of growth.

☞105☜
We cannot understand the profound
influence we have on our children's
lives – or perhaps we don't want to
because it's too frightening.

👎106👍
Pride in your children
is pride in a job well done.

👎107👍
A child's photograph on the wall
is a trophy of parental achievement.

👎108👍
A parent's touch soothes.

🖐109🖐

Sand and water mean adventure to a child,
and a beach is a heaven of exploration.

☞110👍

Every parent can leave their
child a valuable inheritance:
care, love and wisdom.

☞111👍

Television is a good babysitter,
but not a good parent.

☜112☞
Parents are horrified to find themselves using the same broken record – the one that was played in their own childhood.

☜113☞
'May I have a sleepover?'
means a sleepunder for parents.

👎114👍
Sometimes the thought of parenthood strikes fear into us when we think of the enormity of the job that has been entrusted to us.

👎115👍
Winning an argument should never mean more to a parent than winning the child.

☞116☜
Children need imaginary superheroes.

☞117☜
Reward a child's achievement with praise,
and you will build future success.

👎118👍

Parents and teachers form a partnership
in education. They should communicate
with one another.

👎 119 👍

Life is not a lottery, and our
children are not scratch cards.

👎 120 👍

If your child is in pain,
you feel it in your own body.

👎 121 👍

Parenting needs perseverance.

👎 122 👍
Showing that you understand a child's
feelings will feed their inner being.

👎 123 👍
It is hard always
to be a good role model.

☞ 124 ☜
Toys reflect the playthings of society.

☞ 125 ☜
The worst thing about holidays with children
is that they are nothing like the holidays
you enjoyed before you had children.

☞ 126 ☜
Anti-schoolitis is a real ailment.
It is vital to discover its cause.

👎 127 👍

A teenager reminds you of what you
want to forget about your own past.

👎 128 👍

A parent is a rudder in the vast and
stormy ocean of life, offering guidance
and direction. God is the anchor.

129

A child that enjoys reading inhabits many worlds.

👎 **130** 👍

Having children is not a leap in the dark.
It is a leap into the future.

👎 **131** 👍

A family kitchen is full of children's
paintings; and for a doting parent it
is the best art gallery in the world.

👎 **132** 👍

A playground swing is an image
of the role of the parent. We push
our child as high as we can, but they
still come back for another push.

👎 **133** 👍

Consult a teenager –
while they still know everything.

👎134👍
Children have always done
'nothing' or 'just stuff' at school.

👎135👍
If a child is attention-seeking,
give him some attention.

👎136👍
A bullied child needs rescuing.

☞ **137** ☜

Give children paper and pens
and they will represent the world –
but not quite in the way that we see it.

👎 **138** 👍
Waiting in restaurants to get served
in the company of young children is
a lesson in overcoming adversity.

👎 **139** 👍
Faith knows that children
are a gift from God.

👎 **140** 👍
When a child's health is threatened,
the parents are suspended in time.

👎 **141** 👍
Only a very select few can give us
constructive criticism about our own child.

👎 142 👍
Explaining the facts of life to
one's children is embarrassing –
because it all seems so unlikely.

👎 143 👍
Responsibility grows with responsibilities.

👎 144 👍

It is extraordinary the lengths
a two-year-old will go to in order
not to put his shoes on.

👎 145 👍

When children lose control,
they need your control to find it again.

146

For teenagers, uniformity
is social acceptance.

👎 **147** 👍

There is plenty of time for
a house to be tidy – when
the children have left home.

👎 **148** 👍

A disobedient child is not asked to tea.

👎 **149** 👍

Sometimes we need a holiday,
or time off from parenting.

👎 150 👍

The parenting journey is one of the most
arduous and challenging to be taken in life.

👎 151 👍

A child forms character as the thread of his
personality is woven into the family tapestry.

👎152👍

Young children are particularly
fond of using the word 'No'.

👎153👍

Parenting is not a competition with
winners and losers – although sometimes
it feels like it at the school gates.

👎154👍

A baby sleeps peacefully,
but the parent awaits the wake-up call.

👎155👍
Parents have one distinct advantage
when trying to understand their children:
they have *been* young themselves.

👎156👍
Children are limpets on
the rock of their parents.

👎157👍
Children always test boundaries.

👎158👍
Make your expectations of
behaviour very clear; then children
are more likely to meet them.

👎159👍
Undivided attention is a feast for a child.

👎 160 👍

Parents spend the first years of their children's lives teaching them to make good choices. They must then try to trust them to make those choices.

👎 161 👍

God understands parenting. He is one.

👎162👍
Children know they are loved
when we listen to them.

👎163👍
The most comforting words in the
parent's vocabulary: 'It's just a phase.'

👎164👍
Parenting holds hard lessons for us
to learn — and we have to grow up quickly.

👎 166 👍
Teenagers are risk takers,
but they can't always assess the risk.

👎 167 👍
The smell of a baby has been oversold.

👎168👍
My grandmother used to say,
'Please is such a little word,
and Thank you isn't long.'

👎169👍
Difficult children can grow up
to be the nicest adults.

👎 **170** 👍

When the teacher says, 'May
I have a quick word, please?'
– brace yourself.

👎 **171** 👍

Children ask your opinion
in order to formulate their own.

👎 **172** 👍

Love is a four-letter word spelled TIME.

☞173☜
Siblings are the testing ground
for the battles of life.

☞ **174** ☜

Impulsiveness is a natural
state of childhood.

☞ **175** ☜

Getting up for school can cause
early morning stomach aches –
the kind that don't seem to occur
during weekends or holidays.

👎 **176** 👍

A baby's first cry is a joy.
The twentieth begins to wear.

👎 **177** 👍

On car journeys, when children ask,
'How long before we're there?',
the parents are usually praying
the same words.

☜178☞
There is a direct relationship between the amount of pocket money and the price of sweets. It's what economists call the law of demand and demand.

☜179☞
Getting into bed makes a child thirsty.

👎180👍
Only a grandparent can *be* as fascinated
by a child's development as its parent is.

👎181👍
A delicate and precious plant is best placed
in the greenhouse until it is ready to cope
with the elements; just as children are *best*
placed in the protection of a loving family.

182

When the world is awake,
the teenager slumbers.

👎 183 👍

School acts as a great conforming agent. The little individual who goes in often comes out as one of the gang.

👎 184 👍

A line of descending wellington boots tells a family's story.

👎 185 👍

Children often demand 'Yes' when they long for 'No'.

👎186👍
There is usually a favourite Christmas present: the small, cheap trinket at the bottom of the stocking.

👎187👍
Never criticize other people's teenagers. You don't know how yours will turn out.

☞188☜
The sharing of parental experiences
with friends is a great help.

☞189☜
Eating a family meal together
provides a sense of family unity,
and prepares the child for social life.

Most of us learn to suppress the child in ourselves. But parents whizz down the playground slide when no one is looking.

👎191👍

Every time you read with a child,
you are sharing the human experience
and enlarging the size of their world.

👎192👍

Everyone else always
has more pocket money.

👎193👍

A parent is a human being too!

☞ 194 ☜

Birthdays are rites of passage:
another year of growth
and a year less of childhood.

☞ 195 ☜

To children the whole of life is a drama,
and they are the star performers.

👎 196 👍

Children need to know that beyond
bitter arguments and conflict people
still love and care for one another.

👎 197 👍

Teach children how they should live,
and they will remember it all their lives.

FROM THE OLD TESTAMENT BOOK OF PROVERBS

👎 198 👍

When the babies are small,
an uninterrupted night's sleep
is a distant memory of bliss.

👎 199 👍

Teenagers and moderation rarely mix.

👎 200 👍

Teenagers' highest priority
is their social life.

👎201👍

For children, the strange creatures
under the bed do exist. But a parent
can stand between them and their terror.

👎202👍
After a child's birthday party,
the person you most admire is the
class teacher. She has all these
children every day for six hours.

👎203👍
Everyone else always has a later bedtime.

👎**204**👍

It is easy to humiliate a child,
but hard to build their self-esteem.

👎**205**👍

Communication skills are best taught
by spending time in conversation.

👎 **206** 👍
Empty threats undermine
good discipline. Only threaten
punishments you are prepared
to carry through.

👎 **207** 👍
The future of mankind depends
on each individual parent.

👎208👍
Shopping and children
are not a good mix.

👎 **209** 👍

An angry child has no inhibitions.

👎 **210** 👍

There are many wet patches on the road
to potty training – usually on the carpet.

👎211👍
A parent watching a child
perform makes a poor critic.

👎212👍
Photo albums are very selective.
They leave out the *sulks*, *tantrums*
and *misery!*

👎 213 👍
Rebellion and mutiny
belong to the two-year-old.

👎 214 👍
Children love to cook. It's the process
of clearing up that they fail to understand.

👎 215 👍
Teenagers need to be self-centred,
in order to discover their sense of self.

👎216👍

It is not known why teenagers
spend long periods in the bathroom.

👎**217**👍

A good mother's children
show their appreciation.

FROM THE OLD TESTAMENT BOOK OF PROVERBS

👎**218**👍

Living vicariously through your children
is a mistake. They will resent living
for you as well as for themselves.

👎219👍
Children do not always
know how to express themselves.
They speak through their behaviour.

👎220👍
After you, the teacher is the most
influential adult in your child's life.

👎 221 👍
Ideally, new mothers
need their own mothers.

👎 222 👍
In the school playground, a girl
finds a best friend to link arms with.

👎223👍

Forgiveness is a grace
that blesses a family.

👎224👍

A toddler explores objects with all his
senses. Everything is new – and tasty!

☞ 225 ☜

The great birthday cake competition
only exists in the minds of the mothers,
but it is deadly serious for all that!

👎226👍
Through their friends,
teenagers see their own reflection.

👎227👍
When someone else disciplines your
child, it can be an outrage – or a relief.

👎228👍
It's their birthday
and they'll cry if they want to.

☝229☝
Large families are large on love
and joy, but also large on washing,
arguing and spending money!

☝230☝
The local playground becomes a
top social location for toddler and
parent. They both need friends.

👍231👎

The first child must bear the brunt
of the parents' learning curve.

👍232👎

It is wise not to let the sun go down
on your anger. Make up before
bedtime, or resentments will fester.

👎233👍

Small boys are like puppies:
they need to be exercised
on a regular basis.

👎234👍

Raising children is one of life's
greatest challenges – enjoy it!

👎235👍

Always apologize when you are
in the wrong. Then your children
will learn to do so as well.

👎236👍

In a family, it often appears
that nature rather than nurture
has a lot to answer for.

👎237👍

Every child has a talent to
run with. Hand them the baton.

☝238☝

It is a poignant moment when a
child walks through the school gates
for the first time – and the gates of
babyhood close behind them for ever.

☝239☝

The most important person
on a touchline is a mum or dad.

👎**240**👍

Other teenagers can come home at whatever time they want.

👎**241**👍

The extended family provides roots for a child's identity. It gives her a *sense of belonging*.

👎**242**👍

A sense of humour is an essential element in surviving parenthood.

It's remarkable what a child can
make from the inside of a toilet roll.

👎244👍

Most babies travel well to begin with,
but soon make clear their aversion
to changes of location and routine.

👎245👍

Sometimes children act as a
barometer for our feelings: watching
them, we know what mood we are in!

👎 **246** 👍

Teenagers only learn to manage money
by being given money to manage.

👎 **247** 👍

It is a wise parent who can occasionally
admit his or her own failings to a child.

👎**248**👍
Resilience is forged through challenges.

👎**249**👍
Two-year-old temper tantrums
are the first great rebellion of life.

👎**250**👍
An artist begins with wax crayons
and computer paper.

👎 251 👍

There is a fine distinction between
the acceptable T-shirt and a garment
fit for no human habitation.

👎 **252** 👍

When we look at the world through the eyes of a child, we see all over again the beauty of God's creation.

👎 **253** 👍

Children need a clean slate when bad behaviour has been dealt with.

254

There is one fear that continually
lurks in our subconscious mind:
that our child should die before us.

255

How the busy, uncreative parent dreads
the words, 'We have to make a costume'!

👎256👍

Continual sibling arguments wear us to a frazzle. One day they may well be the best of friends, but when will that day be?

👎257👍

When our children are on the verge of adulthood, we are never sure that we have prepared them sufficiently for life.

👎258👍

Giving good gifts to your children
is a delight. Seeing their faces
light up warms the heart.

👎259👍

We cannot protect our children
altogether from the knocks of life, and
it wouldn't do them any good if we did.

260

Young children explore food
as if it is an unknown land.

👎261👍
Children are very adaptable
to the vagaries of their parents.

👎262👍
The good teacher has an alarming
way of summing up our child.

👎263👍
Tomorrow is a long time for a child.

👎 **264** 👍

It's wonderful for a child to
have a grandparent to enthrall
with every small milestone.

👎 **265** 👍

The worst temper tantrums are
invariably thrown in the supermarket.

👎 **266** 👍
Keep calm: hysterical children
can produce hysterical parents.

👎 **267** 👍
It is a difficult and strange adjustment
to make when a child leaves home.
There is an empty space at the table
and in your heart.

👎268👍

The arrival of babies stretches the elastic band of matrimonial love to its full tension.

👎269👍
Those who praise our children,
flatter us.

👎270👍
Toy building blocks
train tomorrow's architects.

👎**271**👍

A child who stays out late
opens the imagination to
the worst possible scenarios.

👎**272**👍

Teenage angst is not easily untangled.
Only time will do the job.

👎 **273** 👍

Children are not afraid of the truth,
but are suspicious of evasion and secrecy.

👎 **274** 👍

One of the great lessons of childhood
is that actions have consequences –
and that they are not all good.

👎275👍

An only child is the prince or princess
of the house, and they rule supreme.

👎276👍

It is wise to get on with your child's teacher.

👎277👍

Kindness to children seeps into their souls.

There are compensations in holidaying with toddlers. You get to build the sandcastle you always dreamed of.

👎279👎
Teenagers need to be asked
to do what needs doing.

👍280👍
Why do schools set homework
that the parents have to do?

☝ **281** ☝
It is best to anticipate bad
behaviour and divert it, rather than
deal with it once it has occurred.

☝ **282** ☝
The gifts of dignity, respect and
self-worth will travel with our children
throughout life, wherever it takes them.

👎**283**👍

The amount of food the teenage boy
consumes is a wonder to behold –
and a strain on the budget.

👎**284**👍

Children need to be seen and heard –
but not every minute of every day.

👎**285**👍

Do not begrudge time spent with your child.

286

A mother and father provide
shelter from the storms of life.

👎**287**👍

When you start offering Ribena
in a beaker to visiting adults,
you are in need of adult company.

👎**288**👍

Raising children is a communal
effort, requiring a network of
neighbours, friends and family.

☟289☝
Parents need to *believe* in their
own authority; otherwise they
will *not be* able to exercise it.

☟290☝
If the adolescent is perturbed by
the radical changes in his personality,
his parents will *be* in a state of shock.

👎291👍

Children must be given the
power to make choices. It's judging
the timing that is the problem.

👎292👍

Children have a natural understanding
and knowledge of the love of God.

👎293👍

Teenagers miss nothing
in sizing up their parents.

Children mould clay into amazing shapes –
shapes that will endure the test of time
on their parents' mantelpiece.

👎295👍

Parents long to give their children
the good things of life. To a child,
parents are the good things in life.

👎296👍

The most trying parent for a teenager
is one who still wants to be one.

☟297☝
Parents know they are flawed.

☟298☝
When children struggle with their school friendships, we can only offer possible strategies. We can't wade in to the playground and sort it out ourselves.

👎 **299** 👍

Children develop weak bladders
on long car journeys.

👎 **300** 👍

The child's mind is full of
fancies we have forgotten.

👎301👍
Never put your first child's compliance
down to brilliant parenting. You may
get a little horror next time around.

👎302👍
Children need our approval
above all other prizes.

👎303👍

Children love games,
especially when adults join in.

👎304👍
Children know parents have buttons
to push – and they will push them.

👎305👍
However strange the garments,
it's the same child inside them.

👎306👍
No parent is perfect.

👆307👍
It doesn't hurt children to wait
a while for what they want.

👆308👍
It is not enough for a child to know
what is wrong and why. She also
needs to know what to do instead.

👎**309**👍
Spending time alone with a child
confirms their importance to you.

👎**310**👍
A child who says, 'It's not fair!' usually
has a brother or sister to contend with.

👎311👍

Friendships forged in mutual
parenthood often last a lifetime.

👎312👍

Children do not notice how deep and high
and wide the mess is, but they do expect
you to be able to locate their belongings.

👍**313**👎

Parents can't help but embarrass
their offspring, but Dad dancing at the
school disco probably wins the top prize.

👎314👍

In the teenage years, peer pressure
is much stronger than parent pressure.
Use your influence while you can!

👎315👍

The first major life crisis is to
become a teenager. This often occurs
just as the parents hit their second.

👎316👍

Parents of a naturally compliant
child take all the credit.

👎317👍

Parents of a naturally strong-willed
child get all the blame.

☜318☞
Children have not yet learned tact.

☜319☞
Parenting is one of the most
expensive pursuits open to humanity.

👎 320 👍

Frustration is not a feeling
that children easily tolerate.

👎 321 👍

Boys have a consistently un-PC
fascination with weapons. They will
make guns out of twigs if nothing
else is available.

👎322👍

Children's volume control is set very high, and they have not yet learned to adjust the sound.

👆323👇
The great outdoors suits children
much better than the small indoors.

👇324👆
Children lack political thought.
That is why they play successfully.

👇325👆
Teenagers have one overriding
anxiety: rejection by their peers.

👎**326**👍

Our commitment to our children is to love them – even when we don't like them very much.

👎**327**👍

Fear for our children's physical safety is a never-ending worry, but wrap them in cotton wool and they will stifle.

👎 **328** 👍

It is the responsibility of the parent
to let the fledgling adult fly.

👎 **329** 👍

Children are a gift from the Lord:
they are a real blessing.

FROM THE OLD TESTAMENT BOOK OF PSALMS

Why is it that wellington boots are not tall enough for the biggest puddles – the ones children choose to jump in?

👎331👍

Compromise and negotiation
are learned skills: parents can
only teach them by example.

👎332👍

Sometime in early parenthood
we make a discovery: our sweet
child is not perfect after all.

👎333👍

Children grow *best* when they
are rooted and grounded in love –
and the family is the compost.

👎334👍

It is wise not to rush to give an answer.
But when you have – stand by it.

👎 **335** 👍

Teenage aggression is best
played out on the sports field.

👎 **336** 👍

Give a teenager a 'No' and they
will beg, plead, argue and rationalize.
The tough part is holding out against
the onslaught.

☞337☜

The child *seeks* approval from the parent,
just as the flower turns towards the sun.

☞338☜

One of the most extraordinary things
about pregnancy is that you are carrying
someone that you will have a lifelong,
intimate relationship with, yet have not met.

Teenagers have their ears pierced
so they can hang telephones off them.

👎 **340** 👍

A good parent raises a gentle child.

👎 **341** 👍

Children only want to carry or ride their belongings on the way to the park. They expect parents to do it on the way back.

👎342👍
Identify your child's strengths,
and you have a prime building site.

👎343👍
Children's bad behaviour dents our own
image – and embarrasses us in public.

👎344👍
Encouragement comes before criticism
if we want our children to move forward.

👎345👍
The unpredictability of children
undermines the routines of adults.

👎346👍
Our children are a major life
priority. If they are not, then
we need to rethink our priorities.

👎347👍

A parent can discover many short cuts around the streets of home – driving a sleepless baby in the car.

👎**348**👍

Parents need to be able to tolerate
being hated (albeit briefly), or
they will be unable to set limits.

👎**349**👍

The toddler's inquisitive nature
leads her naturally to trouble.
When all goes quiet – she's found it.

☞ **350** ☜

If the door hinges survive the teenage years, then the parents probably will.

☞ **351** ☜

Jesus said, 'Let the children come to me and do not stop them, because the Kingdom of heaven belongs to such as these.'

FROM THE NEW TESTAMENT GOSPEL OF MATTHEW

☞**352**👍

We need to give our children the vocabulary
of feelings, and the permission to use it.

☞**353**👍

Pregnant with the second child, one
wonders if it will ever be possible to
love them with the same intensity as
the first. But when they arrive – we do!

👇354👍

Godparents can be a great blessing
to a child. They show that he is valued
outside the confines of the family.

👇355👍

The sparks of adolescent discontent
are easily fanned into a flame by a
chance comment.

👎**356**👍

A *baby's* smile – that unearthly,
toothless grin – is a glimpse of heaven.

👎357👍

Good parenting shows children the
road map of life, warns of dangers and
difficulties – but does not direct the route.

👎358👍

Children do not understand sarcasm.

👎359👍
Children need attention
like plants need water.

👎360👍
Father Christmas gets tired and
emotional waiting for excited children
to fall asleep. He rarely gets a
lie-in in the morning, either.

☝ 361 👍

Parents need a life of their own
as well as looking after children.

☝ 362 👍

The growing child must separate
from the comfort and protection
of the parent in order to stand
strong and healthy on his own.

👎363👍

Children have to be able to leave home
successfully before they can return to have
an adult relationship with their parents.

👎364👍

We are entrusted not just with the
physical well-being of our children
but with the feeding of their souls.

👎365👍

Parents have immeasurable
pride in their newborn, as does
God at the creation of his world.